shark man

RODNEY FOX

An Omnibus Book from Scholastic Australia

W9-CPQ-202

Omnibus Books

52 Fullarton Road, Norwood SA 5067

an imprint of Scholastic Australia Pty Ltd (ABN 11 000 614 577)

PO Box 579, Gosford NSW 2250.

www.scholastic.com.au

Part of the Scholastic Group

Sydney . Auckland . New York . Toronto . London . Mexico City .
New Delhi . Hong Kong

First published in 2001.

Text copyright © Rodney Fox, 2001.

All photographs, except those separately acknowledged, copyright
© Rodney Fox, 2001.

Design copyright © Katrina Allan, 2001.

National Library of Australia Cataloguing-in-Publication entry

Fox, Rodney, 1940- .
Sharkman

ISBN 1 86291 448 6.

1. Fox, Rodney 1940-. 2. Conservationists - Australia - Biography.
3. Sharks - Australia. 4. Shark attacks - Australia. I. Title.

597.310994

Typeset in Dutch766, 10 pt by Katrina Allan.
Printed and bound in China by Everbest Printing Co Ltd.

10 9 8 7 6 5 4 3 2 1   1 2 3 4 5 / 0

To Kay,
A GREAT WIFE AND PARTNER

sharkman

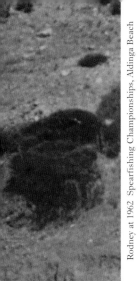

Rodney Fox (left) and Bruce Farley with
their home-made spear guns, 1962.

Weighing in fish during the Spearfishing Championships 1963,
half an hour before the attack.

CONTENTS

1 Shark Attack 2

2 Back in the Water 12

3 The Tiger Shark, Whaler
Sharks, and the Power Head 16

4 Game Fishing, Great Whites,
and the First Underwater Cage 22

5 Blue Sharks and Chain
Mail Death Suits 28

6 The Hammerhead Shark
and Shark Repellent 32

7 Cage Diving with Mini Me,
the Great White 38

Glossary 47

Index 48

shark

IN 1963 I WAS THE REIGNING SPEARFISHING
CHAMPION OF SOUTHERN AUSTRALIA, AND IN
DECEMBER OF THAT YEAR I WAS DEFENDING MY
TITLE. ABOUT 40 SKINDIVERS, THEIR FRIENDS,
AND FAMILIES HAD GATHERED FOR THE
COMPETITION AT ALDINGA BEACH, ABOUT 40 MILES
(65 KM) SOUTH OF ADELAIDE.

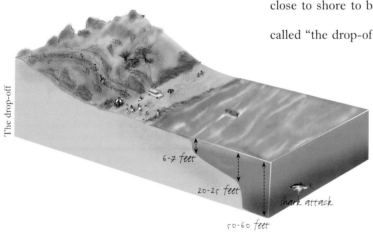

The drop-off

6-7 feet

20-25 feet

shark attack

50-60 feet

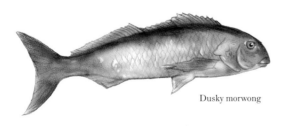

Dusky morwong

A very high cliff separates the sea and the road at Aldinga Beach. A horseshoe-shaped reef is usually exposed along the shoreline. The water goes from about 6 or 7 feet (2 or 3 m) deep close to shore to between 20 to 25 feet (6 to 10 m) at a place we called "the drop-off." Past this the sea floor falls away to about 60 feet (20 m). It was at the drop-off, at about 1 pm on December 8th, that my life changed forever.

The conditions were good for snorkeling. The water was clear and the fish were plentiful. Attached to my belt was a 25-foot (10 m) long rope tied to a float. I had two fish tied to this float with a loop of wire. I dove and swam slowly along the reef, holding my breath, and conserving energy. A large dusky morwong (a large Australasian fish) swam in front of me and I leveled my spear gun and targeted it at the fish. I was just about to fire when a crushing thump on my left side knocked the gun from my hand and the mask off my face. It felt like a train hit me!

attack

THE PRESSURE ON MY CHEST WAS ENORMOUS AND A GREAT GURGLING ROAR FILLED MY EARS AS I WAS HURLED FORWARD THROUGH THE WATER. THE REALIZATION WAS TERRIFYING – IT HAD TO BE A HUGE SHARK!

The force of the water swung my legs back along the shark's immense body. The great beast propelled me through the water faster than I could ever swim, and yet it moved in a slow and relaxed manner.

I remember the awful contrast between those two things. I was a bone in a dog's mouth: the shark would consume me at its leisure.

My mind was racing. What could I do to escape? The shark's eyes were its only vulnerable parts. Its top jaw was clamped right around my back, forcing my left arm up over its body. With my right hand I clawed frantically at its head and eyes.

I WAS A BONE IN A DOG'S MOUTH: THE SHARK WOULD CONSUME ME AT ITS LEISURE.

The great shark released its grip and instinctively I thrust out my right arm to fend it off – and saw it disappear into the monster's mouth! I felt the pain of slicing flesh as the palm of my hand and the underside of my arm ripped across the razor-sharp points of the shark's bottom teeth. I quickly pulled my arm out, before the great creature could close its mouth again. I lifted the limb so high away from the bottom teeth that I dragged it along the top teeth and sliced my flesh to the bone.

Instinctively I bear-hugged the shark, wrapping my arms and legs hard around the massive body so it could not get me. I couldn't get around it because of its bulk – all I could do was hold on to the curve.

Greater than my fear of the shark was my need for air. I had to release my grip, push off towards the surface and kick my way to the top. I gratefully gasped one deep breath, then looked down through the water. This was the most terrifying, unforgettable moment of all. My body floated in a red sea and as I looked down through that bloody water, surging upwards through the reddish haze was an open set of jaws with razor-sharp teeth. The shark was coming back to eat me.

No gun. No knife. No escape. My chest wall was almost severed, my left shoulder blade holed, my hands had deep punctures and lacerations. I had only a second to consider what to do next.

Utterly terrified, I kicked down as hard as I could, my left flipper just grazing the top of the shark's head. Without warning, the monster turned its attack from me to the fish float trailing behind me. It swallowed the float and the fish. Then it turned in a big circle. The float line must have caught in the toothless hinge section in the back of its jaw. Suddenly I was being dragged rapidly through the water. I gulped down one or two frantic breaths before the shark plunged towards the ocean floor. Water gurgled and roared past my ears and over my body. I was spinning uncontrollably like a lure on a line, being towed deeper and deeper.

The rope that was dragging me under was attached to my lead belt, which had a quick-release clip. Subconsciously, I reached for the release mechanism with my left hand. My left arm was also badly cut underneath the triceps muscle, and my fingers grasped at nothing. There was no buckle at my waist.

Through the surging, swirling, spinning nightmare I groped, running fingers along the belt over the lead weights looking for the quick-release.

The little air I had managed to gulp down before being hauled back under the water was almost exhausted. My mind was becoming fuzzier every second. The belt must have slipped around my body, but I could not stretch my arm around my back in a final search for the buckle. I had done what I could. I was about to open my mouth and breathe in water when I felt the line snap.

Normally, that rope would have taken much more strain. When the shark bit me around the chest he must have cut part-way through the rope. When the rope snapped, I had enough encouragement and strength to hold on a little longer, even though I barely knew which way was up.

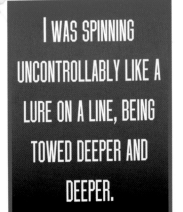

I WAS SPINNING UNCONTROLLABLY LIKE A LURE ON A LINE, BEING TOWED DEEPER AND DEEPER.

I remember "leafing it" – an ascending motion, the reverse of a leaf falling from a tree – and holding on to get to the surface.

Even before I yelled "Shark!", a boat arrived. The alarmed officials had already seen the blood staining the water. I couldn't offer them my lacerated arms – I thought they would pull them off! They had to roll me into the boat, where I collapsed. Then they raced towards shore, hauling another diver from the water on the way.

My rescuers drove a wooden boat right up on to the sharp rocks of the reef. Bruce Farley was the fellow they had picked up on

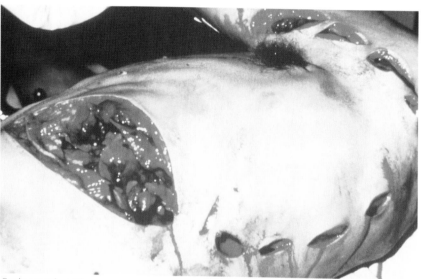

On the operating table

the way in, and he sat up on the bow. He told me afterwards that he didn't think there was much hope for me, and he didn't want to look at me. Blood was pouring out from my wetsuit and I was perfectly white.

On the way, in they asked what they could do for me. I was pretty far gone, but managed to indicate I wanted my flippers off, because my feet were feeling bad.

I didn't know what sort of a shark had attacked me. Later, of course, when we checked the tooth marks on my body and wetsuit there wasn't any doubt at all that it was a great white shark, or white pointer, as it is sometimes called.

I know a lot more about sharks these days. Enough to know that the normal feeding habit of the great white is to grab hold and swing its head around, thus sawing a piece out of what it is biting. Without a doubt, if that shark had ever thought about shaking its head it would have completely finished me off!

Aldinga Beach

Attack site **X**
Boat to reef edge
X Rodney carried to car
Car drove up sandy beach to road

MY LEFT LUNG HAD BEEN PUNCTURED, MY SPLEEN WAS LEFT UNCOVERED EXCEPT FOR A MEMBRANE OVER THE TOP, AND THE MAIN ARTERY FROM THE HEART TO THE STOMACH WAS EXPOSED JUST ALONG THE SIDE OF THE BITE.

If I had been grabbed just an inch to the right, then that would have been it for me. All my ribs on the left-hand side were crushed, and the shoulder blade had a hole through it where a tooth had gone right through the bone.

I was only semi-conscious when they reached shore. In 15 years no one could remember a car having been on that beach, but there was a car waiting on the reef to help me. Frank Alexander, the president of the Spearfishing Association, had decided he didn't want to walk up and down the cliff carrying things for his family that day. The sand had packed just right, and so for the first time ever, Frank had driven his car along the beach. And now he had driven it right over the sharp, pot-holed reef, with no thought to his tires.

As they lifted and rolled me out of the boat, my side, where it had been ripped, gaped open, and loops of my insides slipped out and hung like sausages. They quickly turned me over the other way. Malcolm Baker, another diver in the competition, who had studied first aid for the police exams, held me together. They propped me up and took off down the beach to the hospital.

As soon as the boat had hit the beach, Bruce Farley leapt out. The reef is razor sharp, full of barnacles and sharp shells, yet he ran for a few hundred yards and didn't even get his feet scratched. The first person he saw happened to be a policeman, who immediately called an ambulance.

Meanwhile, in the back of Frank's car, I was being urged to keep breathing. Breathing was my biggest problem, because my collapsed left lung was restricting the air to my good lung. I was trying to suck air into my right lung as hard as I could, while everything on my left side gurgled and spluttered.

My comprehension was minimal. I could hear, but I didn't really know what was going on. One sensation I do recall vividly was the way the back of the car swayed as we sped at 90 miles per hour (150 km/h) down the road.

Somebody put a hand on my damaged chest, and when he took it away I managed somehow to indicate it was better if he kept it there.

Serrated teeth of a great white shark

... IT WAS A BIG, UGLY JOB AND EVERYONE THOUGHT I WOULD PROBABLY DIE ANYWAY.

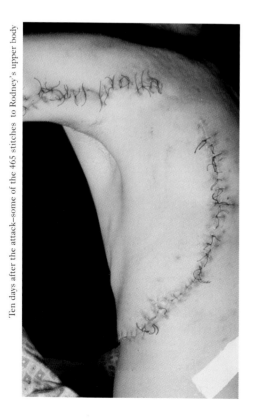

Ten days after the attack—some of the 465 stitches to Rodney's upper body

The hand on my chest stopped the gurgling sounds from the collapsed lung.

I heard the shouts – "Here's the ambulance … Stick a shirt out the window … Hang a towel out." The car screeched to a halt.

I could sense that they were pleased to get me some help. It showed in their voices. I was a mess.

It was a miracle I was still conscious. I fought to keep breathing. Doctors told me later that if I had lost consciousness I would probably have died in the car.

I was transferred to the ambulance and given oxygen. That was probably the real lifesaver of the day, because I had very little blood left. A police escort accompanied me all the way to the hospital. The ambulance drivers, Mrs. Gerkie and Mrs. Bebe, told me later the slowest speed all the way was 45 mile per hour (70 km/h) around one corner.

It is about 40 miles (65 km) from Aldinga to Adelaide. Police manned traffic lights and all the stop signs. It was about 1:30 pm on a Sunday afternoon – the best possible time as far as traffic was concerned. If it had been three hours later, we would not have made it through the traffic.

The time from when I was attacked to the time I reached the hospital was less than an hour. Even five minutes more and all my veins would have collapsed.

The doctor on emergency standby quickly examined me. When he described my massive wounds to two other surgeons at home, they said they were not available. The story I heard years later was that it was a big, ugly job and everyone thought I would probably die. Dr. Justin Miller, the emergency doctor, decided to stitch me up himself.

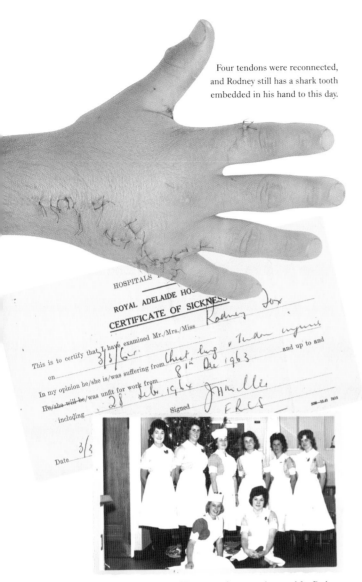

Four tendons were reconnected, and Rodney still has a shark tooth embedded in his hand to this day.

The team of nurses who cared for Rodney

I woke up on the operating table. I was still drugged to deaden my nerves and relax my muscles while the complex repairs and extensive stitching went on. I was not breathing normally, so an oxygen tube had been inserted through my nose into my good right lung. It seemed I was lying in an open coffin with dark sides, looking upwards at a bright light. I felt that light was my life – that if it went out I would be finished. Loud voices were shouting around me. I sensed the panic in the operating room, and the light, my symbol of life, shrank dramatically. The doctors had run out of oxygen in one cylinder so they had to attach another one to re-inflate my right lung.

Pictures of my childhood played in my mind. Stealing marbles from a department store, starting a fire that burned down a neighbor's fence: things I was ashamed of and had hidden from my mother.

GRADUALLY, THE LIGHT GREW STRONG AGAIN AND I FOUND MYSELF TAKING SHALLOW BREATHS. I WAS IN A LOT OF PAIN, BUT I HAD SURVIVED.

Letters from well-wishers

For five days I was in the recovery ward. I had been dosed with every conceivable type of antibiotic because nobody knew just what kind of bacteria was in the shark's teeth. The medical staff expected shock to set in, but it never did. I attribute this partly to my being in good shape at the time of the attack and partly to the fact that I acknowledged a shark attack was a possibility. A lot of shark victims die from shock because they don't think it can ever happen to them.

IN MY MIND I SAW SHARKS ATTACKING FROM ALL DIRECTIONS.

Ten days after the operations I was "unwrapped." The hundreds of stitches were secure, and there was new skin everywhere. I was allowed to go home for Christmas after only two weeks.

While I was in the hospital the subject of spearfishing was not raised, but for me the question was always there. Exploring the sea had been more than a hobby to me – it was a way of life.

Three months after the attack there was a gathering of skindivers at Horseshoe Reef, close to Adelaide. Horseshoe Reef has always appealed to skindivers. In their underwater world, there are spots that definitely feel friendly. Others are equally unfriendly. Kay, my wife, and I sat on the beach for a time and chatted with the other divers. Then Kay paddled me out to the reef, about 100 yards (100 m) offshore. I had my fins and mask and a spear gun for protection. With divers all around me, I slipped into the water and immediately turned my head around.

Rodney brings home the catch

In my mind I saw sharks attacking from all directions. I shook off the sharks with a shake of my head and said to myself, "You are going to have to control that, Rodney, or you won't be any good!" Then I spotted a fish about 16 feet (5 m) below me, its head protruding from a cave. It was all the incentive I needed. The deep breath I took for the dive hurt. I was conscious of pressure and tightness as I swam down. I fired the five-pronged head of the spear, hitting the fish, and came to the surface as proud as I could possibly be.

I was exhausted, but the feeling was wonderful. It was my nature to be the hunter and bring home the catch.

Rodney's wife Kay

'POKED SHARK IN EYES—MADE IT LET GO'

Baits set

Aldinga storekeeper Mr. Ray Ball said to-day that two youths, members of the Knights of Neptune Spearfishing Club, the club to which Rodney Fox belonged, had set five drum lines off the Aldinga beach. The baited drums were set in the vicinity of where Fox was attacked.

Victim tells

"The shark grabbed my body in its mouth. It wouldn't let go. I had to poke my fingers into its eyes to make it release its hold."

This was part of a dramatic account given by skin diver Rodney Fox about his encounter with a killer shark off Aldinga beach yesterday.

Fox was competing in the State Spearfishing Championships when a big bronze whaler shark struck.

He was hauled into a boat suffering from severe chest injuries, a punctured lung and loss of blood.

Only his attractive young wife and his mother were permitted to see him today in Royal Adelaide Hospital, where he is recovering from a life saving emergency operation.

His mother, Mrs. J. X. Fox, of Klemzig, said her son spoke only briefly of the attack.

"Rodney said he was swimming around when the shark attacked," she said.

"The shark's jaws closed over his body and would not release its hold," Fox continued.

"Rodney had to poke his fingers into the eyes of the shark before it would release its grip.

Twine b...

"The shark then let off, circled and made other attack," grabbing a floa...

"Rodney said ... pulled about ... through the ... shark made ... float, but h... when twine ... snapped.

Spearfishe... day it w... divers to ... cable on to ... their fish.

Also ... float was ... which wa... diver so ... catch as ... the water.

Skindi... shark ... the fish ... when it a...

Yesterday's attac... probably cause spear-fishing clubs to stop stag-ing underwater competi-tions off popular southern beaches, Mr. Brian Rodger said today.

Mr. Rodger, a shark at-tack victim himself at Aldinga nearly three years ago, is president of the Knights of Neptune ...

ALL ATT...

9 GNS.
less 4 one ...

...heque
...s Tree, sponsored by The

...toria square by

Rodney Fox pictured in hospital today.

SHARK SWAM WIT ME IN HIS MOUT

"The shark was swimming along in the water with me in his m... d to push him off but my hand went into his jaws. I pulled it a ...gan searching for his eyes . . ."

his was part of a dramatic account spear-...erman Rodney Fox gave today of his battle ... life with a killer shark off Aldinga on Sunday. ... It the ambulance trip to hospital w... a little bit longer. I wouldn'... ...said

"I was floating in on ...
"I didn't k...

...he Sun, Monday, Dec. 9, 1963

...ark grabs man around waist

Will live

RACKS N SA DGE

ADELAIDE, Sun. — A large shark grabbed a young spear fisherman around the waist at Aldinga, 30 miles south o... Adelaide, this afternoon.

The man, Mr Rodney Fox, 23, of Edwardstown, Adelaide, has severe stomach and lung injuries and a mauled right hand.

Doctors worked late into the night in at-tempts to save his life. The attack was only 100 yards from where a shark mauled another spear-fisherman, Mr Brian Rodger, in March last

With Mr Brian Brawley, of Henley, Adelaide, he dragged Mr Fox aboard and sailed fast for a near-by reef.

"We held him in a posi-tion to keep the wounds closed," Mr Francis said.

Mr J. F. Alexander, chairman of the SA coun-cil of underwater activi-...his car on to...

Rodney (left) on the beach before the attack

BACK
IN THE
WATER

I BEGAN TO TRAIN IN THE FRESHWATER SINKHOLES IN THE
MOUNT GAMBIER DISTRICT, WHERE THERE ARE NO SHARKS!

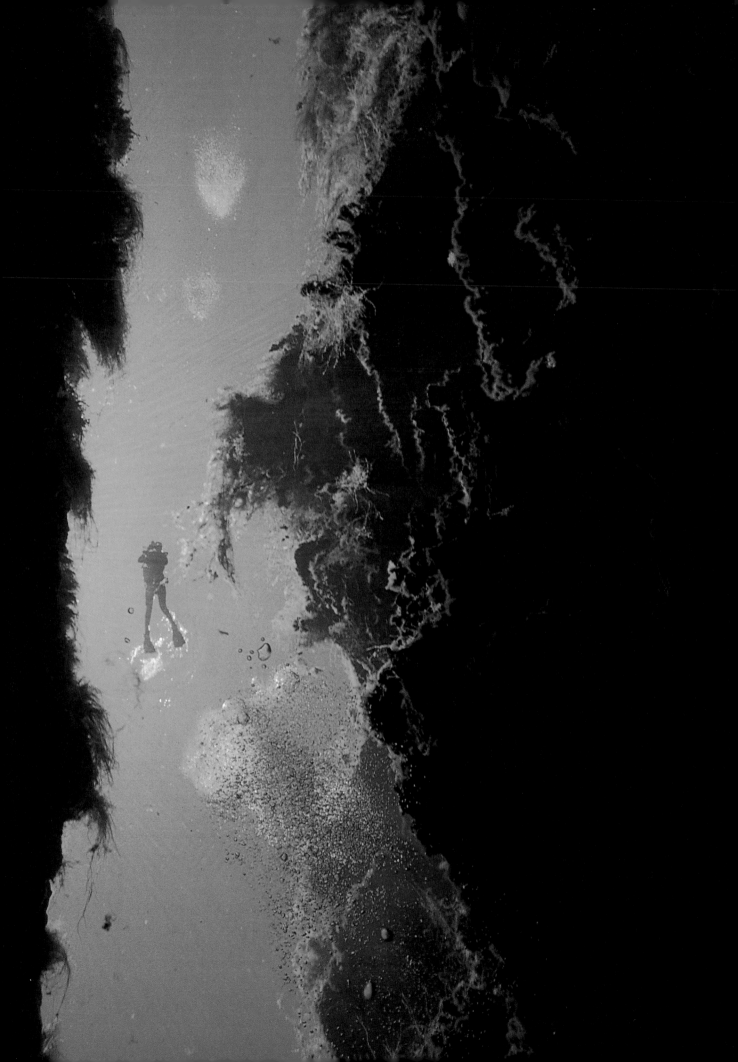

King George whiting

Brian Rodger, Rodney Fox and Bruce Farley, Australian spearfishing team champions in 1964

IT TOOK TIME TO RECOVER FROM BOTH THE PHYSICAL AND THE PSYCHOLOGICAL EFFECTS OF THE ATTACK. I WORKED HARD TO GET PHYSICALLY FIT, BUT MENTALLY – WELL – I WASN'T SO SURE.

Yellowtail kingfish

Blue groper

Lobster

When an opportunity arose to dive with friends the next summer, I accepted. Bruce Farley and Brian Rodger planned a trip to Althorpe Island near Yorke Peninsula, a spot renowned for its blue groper, yellowtail kingfish, and lobsters. I joined the party, but took a fishing rod in case I needed an excuse to stay out of the water!

We anchored in the lee of the island and the others got ready to snorkel, but I wasn't ready. I opted to stay on board and fish for King George whiting.

If a school of kingfish hadn't decided to swim under the boat at that moment, I might have stayed out of the water. Big fish are very rare in southern Australia. One look at those beauties, and I was suddenly ready to dive. Within moments of entering the water I saw a big school of kingfish swim by. Bruce hit one dead center with a beautiful shot. He returned to the boat with his catch, while Brian drifted away in search of the elusive school, which had moved on. I was alone in 65-foot (20 m) deep water – but only for an instant.

FROM DEEP BELOW A HUGE DARK SHAPE CANNONED UPWARDS – IT WAS A BIG SHARK COMING STRAIGHT FOR ME!

From deep below a huge dark shape cannoned upwards – it was a big shark coming straight for me! My heart pounded. I pointed my spear gun, thinking it was never going to stop this shark! Thankfully it didn't need to. The shark must have had second thoughts. It suddenly turned and swam away.

I couldn't get to the surface fast enough. I broke the water shouting, "Shark! Shark!" That was the moment when I might easily have given up diving forever. I wanted desperately to get out of the water, but my arms were still not strong enough to pull myself into the boat. My diving companions had not seen the shark and were less concerned. I had to take refuge between them for the time being.

It was an uncomfortable start. Diving needed to feel a lot safer for me to feel good about it again. I would have to find a weapon that could give me a greater sense of safety underwater. As well, my damaged lung needed time to heal. Deep diving would put great pressure on it, and so I began to train in the freshwater sinkholes in the Mount Gambier district, where there are no sharks! It was after I had managed a successful 90-foot (30 m) dive that I knew I was physically ready. The rest would have to wait.

The Tiger Shark, Whaler Sharks

NOT LONG AFTER THE TRIP TO ALTHORPE ISLAND I MET RON AND VALERIE TAYLOR, BOTH CHAMPION DIVERS AND UNDERWATER PHOTOGRAPHERS. WE DISCUSSED SAFETY UNDERWATER, AND RON SHOWED ME THE EXPLOSIVE .303 POWER HEAD.

The power head is attached to a conventional spear gun. On impact, the .303 bullet is forced on to the firing pin, setting it off: the explosive gases follow, making quite a mess of the shark.

It consisted of a stainless steel barrel and pin, attached to a spear gun. A shell in the chamber explodes on contact with the shark. I suggested we film an expedition where we shot sharks with this new weapon. They knew where to find some sharks.

On one such expedition, Ron and Valerie were in one 13-foot (4 m) aluminium boat and a friend, John Harding, and I were in another. We anchored our boats well offshore in 35 feet (10 m) of water off Flinders Reef in Queensland. We slipped over the side. Ron and Valerie had cameras, John had a spear gun with a conventional barbed head, and I had my spear gun with its .303 power head loaded. There were three extra bullets in my wetsuit sleeve.

and the **Power Head**

ALONE, OUT OF SIGHT OF ANY LAND, WE STARTED FINNING HARD BACK TOWARDS THE REEF.

Grey nurse shark *Photo: David Pearlman*

SPEEDING STRAIGHT AT US OUT OF THE GLOOM LIKE LETHAL TORPEDOES WERE A PACK OF SILVER-GREY SHARKS. ONE IMMEDIATELY ATTACKED THE STRUGGLING FISH JOHN HAD SPEARED. ANOTHER CAME STRAIGHT TOWARDS ME.

While the others filmed fish close to the reef, John and I headed out to look for sharks.

A strong current pushed us along the reef. From the surface we sighted a 10-foot (3 m) grey nurse shark. We yelled for the camera, one arm in the air as we followed the creature. We needed the encounter to be filmed, and we expected at any moment the others would turn up with the camera. When the water got deeper we took turns snorkeling down to keep the shark in sight. It disappeared into very deep water, and we realized we had drifted over a mile along the reef. We could not see our boat at all!

Alone, out of sight of any land, we started finning hard back towards the reef. My legs soon ached, but I quickly adopted a speed

and rhythm that I could keep up for hours, if necessary. We were making slow progress against the powerful current when a school of large silver Spanish mackerel suddenly surrounded us. These very saleable fish had often paid for our gas and food. John dove, aimed, and hit one fish a bit lower than the spine. It was struggling while the school continued to circle us. Something moved into my field of vision, and my stomach churned. Speeding straight at us out of the gloom like lethal torpedoes were a pack of silver-grey sharks. One immediately attacked the struggling fish John had speared. Another came straight towards me. Any closer and I could not have fired my gun. I actually felt the concussion as the spear hit and the bullet exploded, blowing a hole in the shark's head. Muscles twitching, it drifted towards the bottom.

The school of mackerel was nowhere to be seen. John, his knees pulled up against his chest, was thrusting his spearless gun at a shark circling him. I reloaded my gun and shot it. Two other sharks were tearing the speared fish to bits. I hit one on the nose with the end of my gun, and it circled further away, giving me time to reload.

My next shot critically wounded that shark, but now I had only one bullet left. Fortunately, the speared fish had been consumed, and the rest of the sharks moved away quickly. We were alone again in a vast ocean.

THE CURRENT HAD SWEPT US FURTHER AWAY, AND I FOUND MYSELF COUNTING THE RHYTHM OF MY KICKS. FIFTEEN OR 20 MINUTES LATER I FOUND MYSELF SAYING OVER AND OVER AGAIN IN RHYTHM, SAVE THE LAST BULLET FOR YOURSELF.

I couldn't get it out of my mind. John and I had completed two-thirds of the distance back, but I could only see two black dots, which were our boats alongside the small white reef break.

Ron Taylor Productions

Rodney uses a power head successfully on a grey nurse shark.

Then, to the left front side of my vision, something large came into view. A huge, square-headed shark was heading straight for us. I recognized it from textbooks as a tiger shark. It was a man-eater, over 10-feet (3 m) long. I didn't change my rhythm, but I remember saying to myself as I checked my gun and power head, *Save the last bullet for yourself – FORGET THAT!* I didn't care if the shark was just curious and wouldn't attack. It was too close and heading straight at us. I aimed, steadied myself, and fired. *BOOM!* The shark absorbed the shock, remained still for a second or two then arched towards the bottom. John and I dove to see its death struggle on the bottom 50 feet (15 m) below, still hoping Ron and Valerie and the camera would arrive to capture our kill.

It seemed to take forever to reach our boat. When Ron and Valerie finally returned, John and I were too exhausted to speak. We told them later about all the action they had missed.

A HUGE, SQUARE-HEADED
SHARK WAS HEADING
STRAIGHT TOWARDS US ...
A TIGER SHARK, A MAN-EATER

Game Fishing, GREAT WHITES AND THE FIRST Underwater Cage

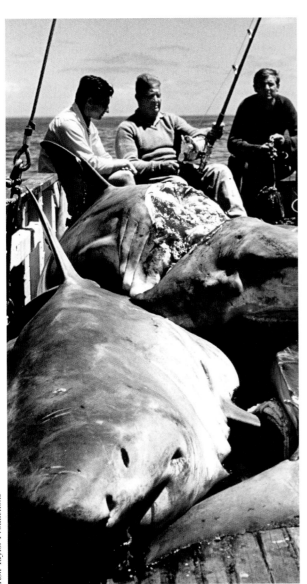

Alf Dean was a well-known Australian game fisherman. He held five world records on rod and line for the capture of great white sharks. His largest, a 2,662-pound (1,208 kg) monster, was caught about 1.2 miles (2 km) out on the remote west coast of southern Australia. Alf had sent me a letter after my attack that played upon my mind.

"IF YOU HAD SEEN WHAT I HAVE," SAID ALF, "YOU WOULD NEVER USE YOUR UNDERWATER GEAR AGAIN. QUIT WHILE YOUR LUCK'S IN, BECAUSE YOU MAY NOT BE SO FORTUNATE WITH YOUR LIFE NEXT TIME!"

I met with Alf and listened to his description of how savage and unpredictable the sharks can be. It made me think that the only way I could learn more and have a good look at these sharks underwater was to protect myself inside a steel cage.

I had made friends with two other shark attack victims. They wanted to see their attackers just as much as I did. A great white had attacked Brian Rodger 18 months before my attack, also at Aldinga Reef. Henri Bource had lost his leg to a great white while swimming with sea lions, a year after my attack. I decided to make a cage that two divers could stand in. I heard stories about monster sharks squashing lobster pots, attacking boats, and biting pieces out of surfboards, and so decided on 1/2-inch (1cm) diameter steel rods welded across each other to form 6-inch (15 cm) squares. An engineering shop built it, 24 inches (60 cm) deep by 68 inches (120 cm) wide by 90 inches (230 cm) high, with finer mesh for the floor and a hinged mesh lid for getting in and out.

Henri Bource (left), Alf Dean and Rodney, with Alf's catch

Ron Taylor Productions

I HAD HEARD STORIES ABOUT MONSTER SHARKS SQUASHING LOBSTER POTS, ATTACKING BOATS, AND BITING PIECES OUT OF SURFBOARDS ...

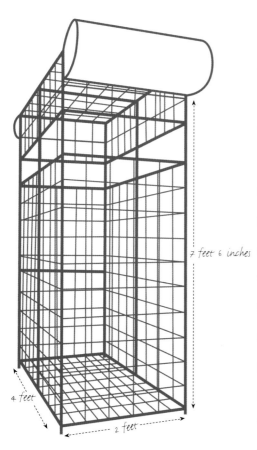

7 feet 6 inches

4 feet

2 feet

Rodney built the first shark cage to view and film great whites underwater. (Side view, showing pontoons to help the cage float.)

This cage could be lowered to water level and tied off with strong ropes to the side of the boat. I cut out some of the mesh bars at eye level, to provide a clearer view and a space for filming.

We arranged to go out with Alf Dean on a tuna boat, the *Glenmorry*. We wanted to get a close view of the giant sharks that had caused us so much trouble. Weary after hours of pounding in rough seas, we anchored behind Wedge Island and put a whale oil slick over the side to lure sharks. No luck. The next day we traveled to calm Memory Cove, where Alf had a lot of success previously.

Once at anchor, we quickly put some fish carcasses over the side, and Alf started his whale-oil slick. In the early hours of the next morning we heard a big bump on the hull. Alf raced outside. In the beam of the floodlight on the stern we saw a very large great white shark swimming around the back of the boat. We put a little more bait over the side to keep it hanging around until morning.

After a hurried breakfast, Alf got his big game rod ready. The shark was swimming about 20 feet (7 m) away from the boat – nowhere near the baited hook. We put the shark-proof cage over the side, determined to take the first underwater film of a great white. I threw out two more fatty baits to lure it closer. Henri hopped into the cage and immediately the shark raced in, had a look at him and made three or four close passes before taking the hookless bait close to the cage and swimming off. I was surprised at the careful way this big shark swam around, very wary until it had the bait in its mouth. Then it went crazy, shaking its head aggressively, and swam off. Henri was almost speechless with excitement.

It was my turn. Nervously, I lowered myself in and dropped under the water. As my feet touched the bottom of the cage I steadied myself by sticking my fingers through the mesh and holding on. The cold water and anticipation made my heart beat

IT WAS LIKE A DEADLY SILVER-GREY SUBMARINE MOVING SILENTLY AND STEADILY THROUGH THE WATER ...

Underwater cameraman Ron Taylor and Rodney made the first film of great white sharks on this 1966 expedition.

faster. On my left a large dark shape emerged around the stern of the boat and quickly disappeared again. A few moments later the great white came up on me from the right. I swung my head and body around to get a good look, at the same time pulling my fingers from the mesh and stepping to the back of the cage. The shark looked enormous as it swam along side of boat and around the cage. Its big black eye seemed to be watching me. I could have reached out to touch it – but I didn't dare. It was like a deadly silver-grey submarine moving silently and steadily through the water, its big tail hardly moving. Its huge mouth opened and gulped on the piece of liver with the hook inside. I surfaced quickly to watch the action on the deck. Alf ordered the skipper to raise the anchor and keep the stern in the direction the shark was going, so that it wouldn't wind the line around the boat. He was already in his game chair and the shark was pulling line off the reel fast. It was 45 heart-stopping minutes before he had the shark alongside the boat and stuck with specially prepared big stainless steel gaffs, with strong rope securing it to the bulwarks.

DANGEROUS REEF HAS A COLONY OF SEVERAL HUNDRED RARE AUSTRALIAN SEA-LIONS ... WHITE SHARKS APPEARED REGULARLY AROUND THE AREA SEARCHING FOR YOUNG PUPS ...

Hauled up on deck by the boat's winch, it proved to be a 4-metre white pointer. Alf said it would probably weigh 1,100 pounds (500 kg). Brian and Henri and I marveled from close range at its fantastic set of sharp teeth, amazed at having escaped in our individual encounters. I imagined my whole chest clamped in similar jaws.

As we were examining the catch another fin appeared – an even bigger shark, a female, swimming back and forth at the stern of the boat. Immediately we re-baited the hook and threw it over, and within minutes Alf had this much larger shark hooked. We were very pleased with the day's work.

Early the next morning we headed off to Dangerous Reef, a horseshoe-shaped rock formation about 19 miles (30 km) from Port Lincoln. Dangerous Reef has a colony of several hundred rare Australian sea lions. Alf believed white sharks appeared regularly around the area searching for young pups, or the afterbirth that gets washed off the rocks in the breeding season.

Rare Australian sea-lions

Dangerous Reef

After dripping whale oil from the stern, and trailing carcass baits over the side on ropes, Brian, Henri, and I decided to have a snooze on the deck. It was a nice, sunny day, and we didn't really expect sharks, having already caught more than we expected to see for the whole 10-day trip.

Just after midday there was a sudden bang at the stern. A big shark had come in, chewed off half the baits quietly and, having had a bit of trouble with the last one, was banging against the side of the boat. We very quickly raised the anchor and put another lure over the side. Alf had the shark hooked and was fighting it when we saw another fin to starboard. I raced to the crow's nest.

The great white shark turns its eye to protect it when it attacks.

There were four sharks in the area! Alf brought the first one alongside, hooked it up and brought it aboard. Sharks were snapping and biting at anything all around the boat. Alf landed two more and was securing one still alive alongside the boat when another shark attacked it. In 15 to 20 seconds of shaking and biting, this shark took out about 90 pounds (40 kg) of flesh from around the head and gills of the captured shark. The ferocity and the huge amount of damage made my stomach churn.

WHEN WE LATER EXAMINED THE BITES WE FOUND THAT THE SHARK HAD CHEWED THROUGH THE JAW – A VERY STRONG CARTILAGE – AND THROUGH THE SPINE, TEARING EASILY THROUGH THE TOUGH SKIN. THE SHARK ITSELF HAD BECOME A SHARK VICTIM.

Ron Taylor Productions

Rodney (left), Brian, and Henri examine another shark victim.

For the three of us, it really brought home the terror of shark attacks. Examining the damaged shark's mouth closely, we found another shark's tail hanging out. In its efforts to throw the hook, this shark had also thrown out a lot of the food it had previously eaten.

On that trip I saw more than enough of the power, frenzy, and ferocity of great white sharks. But we had excited these sharks by putting carcasses, whale oil, and fish into the water. We had not seen them in their natural, unprovoked state. I had a great deal more to learn about these magnificent creatures.

Blue Sharks

and the Chain Mail

AS MY UNDERSTANDING OF SHARKS AND THEIR BEHAVIOUR GREW I BEGAN TO BELIEVE THAT NEITHER FEAR NOR FUN WAS A GOOD REASON TO KILL SHARKS. IT SEEMED TO ME THAT THEY HAD AS MUCH RIGHT TO LIVE AS I DID. I DID NOT WANT VENGEANCE AGAINST SHARKS BECAUSE OF MY ATTACK. I WAS ASKED MORE FREQUENTLY TO PARTICIPATE IN DOCUMENTARIES AND SCIENTIFIC STUDIES. EACH EXPEDITION TAUGHT ME MORE, BUT ON ONE, I AGAIN CAME VERY CLOSE TO LOSING MY LIFE, AND THIS TIME IT WAS NOT A SHARK THAT THREATENED ME.

D r. Eugenie Clark, Professor of Zoology at Maryland University, USA, and I were co-stars in a big screen IMAX film production called *Search for the Great Sharks*. It included diving with whale sharks, great whites, and blue sharks.

I was asked to try out a shark-resistant chain mail suit and hand-feed a blue shark with a mackerel. The chain mail suit went on over my wetsuit and was so tight and inflexible it had to be taped at the elbows and knees to allow movement. I had to have someone help me put on my scuba tank and fins. Our boat was drifting over the 3,200-foot (1000 m) deep channel between the coast of California and the Catalina Islands, a two-person shark cage hanging 10 feet (3 m) under the boat.

Death Suit

Up to twelve 8-foot (2.5 m) blue sharks were following our berley trail. The cameraman, director, and safety diver all took their places underwater and Dr. Clark and I swam down and entered the open-front shark cage. I couldn't operate the radio communications in my full-face mask, hold on to the cage, and feed fish to sharks at the same time. I had thought the weight of the 26 pound (12 kg) stainless steel suit would be enough without a lead belt, but I was much too light. The safety diver swam up to the surface and brought back four 4.5-pound (2 kg) weights, which he put into the pockets of my buoyancy jacket. I could see about eight blue sharks circling in the clear water. The huge camera was in position, with the safety diver swimming behind the cameraman, his shark prod ready to protect him. A big blue shark circled closer and headed straight towards the fish in my gloved hand. The hair on my neck prickled; the shark was very close now. This was it! One bite and half the fish was gone. Two bites, just the tail was left. IMAX film is very expensive and every scene must count! I had to try to keep the action going for at least 20 seconds.

The full-face mask *Photo: Chuck Davis*

MY CLENCHED FIST WAS IN THE SHARK'S MOUTH. I FELT THE TEETH CRUNCHING ON THE CHAIN MAIL

Photo: Chuck Davis

Rodney is helped into the chain mail suit.

The third bite came after only three seconds of film time and my clenched fist was in the shark's mouth. I felt the teeth crunching on the chain mail. If my chain mail fist caught in the shark's jaws my elbow or shoulder could be dislocated as the shark swam off.

I could have been dragged out of the cage. With my right arm I grabbed the shark around the back and belly, stopping it from swimming away as I dragged my hand from its snapping jaws. The shark was now struggling madly and pointing into the cage. It might knock us around if I let go, so I wrestled with it for a moment before it swam off. Everyone gave me the thumbs up. This was just what the director wanted!

The next day as I entered the water one of my flippers came off and sank fast. I dove down 30 feet (10 m) and caught it, but the steel suit was so tight I could not bend to put it on again. I was over weighted, sinking fast, and my ears were aching. Feverishly I kicked with my left flipper to try to get to the surface. The cage and boat were drifting out of sight and two blue sharks began circling me. I was wearing an unfamiliar full-face mask and found it was difficult to equalize the pressure in my ears with the nose press. I was still sinking and, with my ears only partially clear, I urgently tried to reach the inflator button on my buoyancy jacket, but it was floating unsecured out of reach above my shoulder. Frantically I kicked backwards and sideways, my reach restricted by the chain mail suit.

I had been taped into the ill-fitting suit and could not get out of it. My ears were enormously painful, and I was breathing very fast. I tried to clear them again and suddenly remembered the four lead weights in the pockets of my buoyancy jacket. With clumsy fingers covered with chain mail I groped to locate the pocket opening. Still sinking I discarded two, three then four weights, but I had sunk too deep and my wetsuit had become compressed. I was still sinking - and I knew the bottom was 3,200 feet (1,000 m) below.

FRIGHTENED AND PANIC-BREATHING I SUDDENLY REMEMBERED I HAD RADIO COMMUNICATION WITH THE SURFACE. I PRESSED THE BUTTON ON THE FACE MASK AND CRIED OUT, "HELP ME! HELP ME! I'M IN TROUBLE!" NO ANSWER. I WAS TOO DEEP.

The depths below were death-black. At the surface I saw light and life. I had to do something or I would die. In a wild rage, I shook my body sideways, my scuba tank heaving from side to side. My buoyancy jacket, attached tightly with velcro around my stomach and chest, moved. Perhaps I could take my tank and jacket off, turn the jacket around and reach my inflator. This was my last chance! I ripped at the velcro belt and shook the tank again. I knew if I dislodged the seal of my full-face mask even a little I would die within seconds. The pain in my head was so severe I was close to blacking out, but I felt the tank come off my shoulders. I groped around for the inflator button and

Buoyancy jacket

Inflator button

couldn't feel it, but I heard the air racing into my buoyancy jacket and kept squeezing that spot. The tank and jacket lifted, and I held on tight as I began to rise. I was moving up faster and faster. Air was rushing out of my mouth from my lungs as well as from the jacket. There were roaring bubbles all around me, and I knew I was coming up too fast, but I didn't care. At least I would be on the surface. The pain in my ears began to reduce. I didn't have to breathe, as the air expanding in my lungs was racing out my mouth.

I broke through the surface almost up to my waist. The sky was blue, with little puffy clouds, and the sun was shining. It was wonderful. My nose was bleeding, my eyes were bloodshot and my ears sore and ringing, but I was alive. Using unfamiliar equipment in the wild without testing it first has nearly killed me on several occasions. Now when a new idea or stunt is suggested I think about it seriously! Recently for a National Geographic documentary I was asked if I would like to drive a prototype "shark-proof" underwater scooter in over 110 feet (35 m) of water with five great whites circling. "A grand adventure and good for the film," the director said. I wondered how many lives I had left. My answer was, "No thank you."

The Hammerhead
and
Shark Repellent

SHARKS HAVE ELECTRO-RECEPTORS CALLED AMPULLAE OF LORENZINI. ELECTRONIC PULSES CAN SEVERELY AFFECT THESE RECEPTORS. STILL SEARCHING FOR A WAY TO PROTECT MYSELF AND OTHERS FROM SHARKS, I WAS HAPPY TO LEAD A SCIENTIFIC EXPEDITION TO TEST A RANGE OF ELECTRONIC PULSES THAT WOULD FLOW FROM ONE ELECTRODE TO ANOTHER.

The spots, or jelly-filled pores on the shark's head are called ampullae of Lorenzini. *Photo: Jeff Rotman*

If successful this electronic shark repellent was expected to protect divers, surfers, and swimmers from shark attack. A large numbers of sharks gather at Osprey Reef in the Coral Sea many sea miles offshore from Cairns, Queensland, Australia. Our team headed out from Cairns in a charter boat for a long overnight trip to Osprey Reef.

Mid-morning the next day we dropped anchor on the reef with the stern of our boat hanging in deep water. As the electrical engineer and scientists worked on their equipment, the divers in our team went to check if there were any sharks in the area. The warm blue water was clear, but neither the bottom nor the reef was visible. With the other divers, I followed the anchor chain down quite a way before the great wall of the reef became visible.

Shark

The *Falie* is often used for scientific expeditions

Two whitetip reef sharks swam along the coral wall. Whitetip and blacktip reef sharks were patrolling along the drop-off. I counted 10 or 11 whitetip, and seven of the faster moving blacktip.

These were relatively harmless sharks. I felt relaxed: my video camera, with its solid aluminium housing, would be useful if a curious or aggressive shark came too close. I could bang it on the nose or jam the heavy housing into the mouth. We continued down the anchor chain to 160 ft. (50 m) with no bottom to the reef wall in sight.

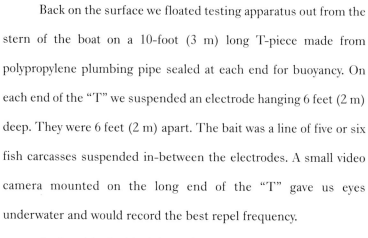

INTO MY VISION CAME A NUMBER OF THE MORE AGGRESSIVE GREY REEF SHARKS, SWIMMING FAST TOWARDS US. I FILMED AS THEY CAME CLOSER AND CIRCLED, BUT WITHOUT ANY BAIT THEY WERE ONLY BRIEFLY CURIOUS.

Monitoring the experiment

Back on the surface we floated testing apparatus out from the stern of the boat on a 10-foot (3 m) long T-piece made from polypropylene plumbing pipe sealed at each end for buoyancy. On each end of the "T" we suspended an electrode hanging 6 feet (2 m) deep. They were 6 feet (2 m) apart. The bait was a line of five or six fish carcasses suspended in-between the electrodes. A small video camera mounted on the long end of the "T" gave us eyes underwater and would record the best repel frequency.

As the whitetip, blacktip, and grey reef sharks came to eat the suspended fish bait, the researchers turned on the current and the sharks would dart away. At times we had a dozen sharks circling, tearing into the bait. We continued to test over several days until it was decided to see if the chosen power and frequency would shock humans. We had to attach another gauge to our floating test bed and wire it back to the computers.

Six divers suited up, and the current to the experiment was turned off until the new gauge was in position. I was the first to jump in. My bubbles cleared in a split second, and I could clearly see

The apparatus, with video camera on the 'T' piece

the baited equipment about 60 feet (20 m) away. Three small blacktip sharks and a big barracuda, almost as long as the sharks, were looking at our fish frames. I was about to up-end and dive clear of the surface slop to make way for the other divers when from the side of my narrow field of vision, closer than my eyes were focused, slid a huge grey shape that blocked my view. My heart beat faster and my chest felt restricted. It was a big hammerhead shark, at least 13 feet (4 m) long. I took out my mouthpiece and yelled above water, "Hammerhead!" I dove under the boat and started filming. I saw one, two, three, four bodies with legs and fins appear underwater at the stern of the boat, their heads out of the water – the divers were probably clearing their masks and getting their cameras. Oh, no! They were completely oblivious of the situation. The shark, attracted by the kicking fins and legs, was swimming aggressively. It passed so close to the others I thought they were goners, but it swam towards our equipment. The divers had no idea how close the shark had been or how easily it could have bitten off a leg or two.

THE DIVERS HAD NO IDEA HOW CLOSE THE SHARK HAD BEEN OR HOW EASILY IT COULD HAVE BITTEN OFF A LEG OR TWO.

The big shark ripped three fish off the apparatus, swallowing them whole. It circled wide, returning with a school of large barracuda streaming after, took another bait fish and turned very sharply to bite the powerless electrodes. I was at the same level in the water, filming, when it headed right for me. I expected the shark to veer right or left but its course was unmoved. As I recorded its approach the hair on the back on my neck stood up. I was the target. The broad hammer-shaped head moved up, and the bottom jaw gaped, exposing dozens of pointed white teeth.

It was within a few feet of me, closing in fast and about to bite. I had thought about this moment hundreds of times before. I had talked about it and told people what to do. I propelled myself forward to meet this attack. My brain said, "Now," and I thrust my aluminium video camera housing out, belting the shark hard on the nose, my arms stiff and my hands clear of the teeth.

I FELT THE THUMP AS THE HEAVY CAMERA MADE CONTACT WITH THE SHARK'S HEAD, BENDING IT BACK A LITTLE AND OPENING THE JAWS EVEN WIDER.

The shark's body pushed me back. I kept the camera stiff in front of me, and turned my body so the shark pushed past me on my left side. It was so close I could see its extra high dorsal fin and the scars from past battles. As it circled rapidly back towards me, I kept my camera in front and pulled my legs up close to my chest. I thrust at it again, but this time it was too far away and my arms were fully outstretched before I could hit it. The shark flinched, but continued circling very close. I was breathing fast and turning with it, wondering if this would ever end, when it moved toward the other divers, then slowly disappeared from view.

THE SHARK FLINCHED, BUT CONTINUED CIRCLING VERY CLOSE. I WAS BREATHING FAST AND TURNING WITH IT, WONDERING IF THIS WOULD EVER END ...

The school of barracuda streamed off following him down, down, down. All of the other divers had witnessed the event, and we very quickly completed our additions to the experiment. On the boat, the scientists could not even try the shark repellent, as it was still disconnected!

Later we watched the video of the incident. Most divers hadn't seen a giant hammerhead before. I wondered why it had picked on me. Had I done anything to promote the attack? Most certainly it had been attracted by the smell of our fish bait. It had eaten three of the bigger baits, stimulating its taste for food. I was the closest diver, and was also on the same level. Many similar shark attacks have occurred when divers feed sharks.

Our tests with the electronic frequencies for a shark repellent were very encouraging, but were not complete. The final product promises to be a worthwhile invention.

AFTER NEARLY 40 YEARS OF SHARK ADVENTURES, AND WITH A GREAT DEAL OF UNDERSTANDING OF THESE CREATURES, I CAN LOOK BACK ON MANY HIGHLIGHTS. ONE WAS BEING CHOSEN BY JAPANESE TELEVISION NETWORK NHK TO PARTICIPATE IN A SERIES CALLED "SUPERTEACHERS." THIS PROGRAM INCLUDED NELSON MANDELA AMONG OTHER SPECIALIST TEACHERS.

Cage Diving
WITH MINI ME,
the Great White

Expedition ship *Falie*

Each "super teacher" was to give lessons to a group of students in his or her particular area of expertise. In my case, six young people representing the children of Australia were to be taught to scuba dive in order to participate in a 10-day great white shark expedition on the *Falie*.

Our first destination was Hopkins Island, near Port Lincoln. I wanted my students to dive with Australian sea lions. The four girls and two boys set off in the ship's tender (a small boat) together with the film crew.

CONDITIONS WERE ROUGH, BUT AS WE ANCHORED, FRIENDLY SEA LIONS SLIPPED INTO THE WATER TO GREET US. QUICKLY WE PUT ON OUR FINS, MASKS, AND SNORKELS AND BEGAN SWIMMING WITH THEM. SOME WERE TWICE AS BIG AS HUMANS, YET THEY SWAM WITH INCREDIBLE AGILITY.

A curious and playful sea-lion encounter

Sea lions leapt right out of the water around us. My students were having a very close and spirited wildlife encounter.

There were sea lion heads, human heads, sea lion fins, and dive fins bobbing and splashing in the water. I anxiously looked for the neoprene hoods of my six students among what seemed to be a mass of sea lions and human bodies. The students were having an exciting time, but I was a little concerned – we were swimming in the sharks' restaurant, and the chances of being their meal were on my mind! We finished off with a scuba dive with these amazing mammals. When the students climbed back on the boat, they were so full of adrenalin that they had forgotten the seasickness, cold, and their fears.

WE WERE SWIMMING IN THE SHARKS' RESTAURANT, AND THE CHANCES OF BEING THEIR MEAL WERE ON MY MIND!

THE FOOD CHAIN

Laura Williams and Ty Kamines *Photo: Von Milner*

We moved on to Grindal Island to complete the number of dives the students needed to qualify for their scuba diving certificates. The rolling motion of the boat set one girl's motion sickness off again and she had to fly home before the trip was complete. We were heading well offshore, and the inclement weather was not expected to improve. With the remaining five students, our expedition boat *Falie* headed south towards the North Neptune Islands, about 38 miles (64 km) away. Five hours later we anchored in a protected bay and started our shark-attracting process. We poured a small stream of minced tuna, tuna oil, and sea water over the side, allowing the tide and winds to take the fishy odor-trail. Any great white shark that came across the trail would be led to our boat, where it would find two tuna fish suspended on ropes just under the water.

The North and South Neptunes are the best places in Australia to find great white sharks, because of the thousands of New Zealand fur seals that breed in the area. While we waited for the sharks to arrive, below deck I began an ecology lesson. I explained that great white sharks were an "apex" predator, because no other fish, shark, or mammal eats them, except perhaps bigger great whites. They are literally at the top of the food chain.

The children had nearly completed their illustrations of the food chain in their logbooks when *Baaarp, Baaarp, Falie*'s horn sounded. Everyone raced upstairs to the stern. A great white had made a couple of passes at the bait. All eyes searched the water and one or two minutes later a large grey shape headed towards one of the tuna baits.

As apex predators – at the top of the food pyramid – sharks help maintain the complex balance of nature in ocean ecosystems. Sharks play an important role when they prey on and check fish and mammal populations. If left unchecked, these populations would increase and deplete their food source, causing whole ecosystems to collapse.

The 13-foot (4-m) shark turned on its side exposing its white belly and pectoral fin and with one gulp ate the 6.5 pound (3 kg) tuna, severing the rope easily.

There were howls and excited laughter from our five nervous, yet excited adventurers. The shark spun and turned for the second floating tuna, swimming close under the boat.

Over the next couple of hours several great whites visited the boat. My son Andrew is a scientist, and he had joined the expedition to conduct a tagging program to study these protected mammals. The two eldest students, a boy and a girl, volunteered to climb down the ladder to stand with Andrew and me. We stood at water level on a platform under the stern of *Falie* and tagged one of three large sharks that were circling. Two had been tagged on a previous trip and swam under the platform, attracted by our bait. They looked much larger at this close range, and everyone felt quite vulnerable. I tried to offer the untagged shark a tuna to get it to come close enough for Andrew to put a tag in its back muscle. Ty and Laura, two of the students, were holding their instant cameras as they stood ankle to knee deep in the surging water.

Our wet feet were growing cold before the opportunity came. The shark moved to take the floating tuna and I slowly pulled the rope towards me. The big shark's head turned as it followed the fish. It was only a foot and a half (1.5 m) from the platform, its large dorsal fin out of the water, when Andrew pulled back the rubber on his tagging pole and fired.

THERE WERE HOWLS AND EXCITED LAUGHTER FROM OUR FIVE NERVOUS, YET EXCITED ADVENTURERS.

THE STAINLESS STEEL TIPPED TAG WITH ITS WHITE NUMBER C7 ENTERED INTO THE SHARK. CAMERAS FLASHED, THE SHARK HIT THE PLATFORM, AND WHITE SPRAY WET US ALL AS THE SHARK'S TAIL SWOOSHED HARD TRYING TO GET CLEAR.

Andrew tags C7

We were close enough to touch it. The students squealed in excitement. As they climbed the ladder to a safer, more comfortable viewing area on deck, their hearts must have been beating hard. This newly tagged shark would help us learn more about the little known distribution and habits of these big predators.

Three great whites had been taking an occasional tuna bait and swimming around the boat since early morning. With the two cages floating at the stern, I prepared to giant-stride into the top of one, dragging a cloud of bubbles down to the cage floor with me. As the bubbles rose to the surface they blocked my view for quite a few seconds. The cold water combined with controlled breathing through a regulator and the sense of pressure made my senses reel. My eyes swept the waters looking for a shark.

The seabed was not visible, and there was only enough visibility in front of me to show the tuna bait with a cloud of small bait fish gathered around it. My eyes searched the clouds of fish clustered in strange shapes under the boat, attracted by our stream of berley. There were no sharks. At the surface three of the girls were getting into their scuba gear. They were nearly ready, and so I signaled OK and went to the end of the cage out of the way. A little fearful, they each stepped off the dive platform with elbows together holding their masks in place, and plunged through the top of the cage. As the bubbles cleared they regained their balance and settled down. One by one they gave me the universal OK sign with their hands and held on to the aluminium mesh, peering through the big camera

slots. I knew what they were looking for. Then, with a big clang that made us all jump, the aluminium door on the top of the cage was closed and we were pushed clear of the platform and away from the boat. Our cage floated on its own, attached to *Falie* by only two manila ropes. The cameraman and his safety diver were in another cage close by to capture all the action on film.

Our cage rocked like a ride in a fun park, but this was no game. This was the real thing! We had been comfortable on a large steel boat looking down into the water at these big predators as they swam close to the boat. Up there our vision was greatly restricted by the rippling surface and the reflected clouds and sunlight, but here in the cage it was different. We were in their world, much closer and not so brave.

A large grey shape emerged out of the blue water. It was a great white in a hurry, and was close to the cage before anyone saw it. I tapped Laura on the shoulder and pointed. We saw Tori and Sarah jump. Instinctively they let go of the mesh and pushed back, bouncing off Laura and me as they lost balance in the rocking cage. The big shark, nearly 16 feet (5 m) long and at least 1,800 pounds (800 kg) in weight, swam smoothly, its great tail moving slowly, yet it rapidly executed a half-circle around our cage. Its big black eye followed us. Then, it saw the tuna hanging on the rope close by. The shark changed course, swam past the fish, looked at it, rejected it and disappeared into the blue. The three girls turned, and I saw the surprise in their eyes. Tori held her hands out wide, and I knew she was saying, *"They are sooooooo biiiiiigggggg!"*

... TWO SMALLER GREAT WHITES SLOWLY CIRCLED BELOW US PERFORMING A STRANGE BALLET. IT WAS LIKE BEING IN A HUGE BLUE-DOMED THEATRE.

A few minutes later two smaller great whites slowly circled below us performing a strange ballet. It was like being in a huge blue-domed theater. The sun's rays piercing the ripples of the surface looked like moving spotlights. These majestic creatures with pectoral fins 10 feet (3 m) from tip to tip were putting on a fine display, flying up, down, and around and around with grace and beauty until they disappeared from sight. It was incredible.

The girls became more confident and moved around the cage so that they could see better. They were now more relaxed and were talking to each other in sign language. Things changed when, with a rush, one medium-sized 11-foot (3.5m) shark came close. It opened its huge cavernous mouth and enveloped the tuna, severing the rope in one bite. Its powerful tail thrust a pressure wave of water through our cage as it swam off.

Andrew, on deck, replaced the tuna and balloon on the line and threw it out. The girls were getting cold and started to move up and down to keep warm, bobbing around, sometimes lying on the floor looking down through the mesh towards the seabed. Soon a much smaller great white started circling. The tuna bait had floated very close to our cage. The shark was circling, building up courage to come and grab the fish. The girls stood by the mesh holding on to the viewing ports and watched through the large clear gaps made especially for big cameras. The shark made several passes, swerving away at the last minute then, with a convincing rush, headed straight for the tuna and us.

Normally, we don't see many small great whites, especially when there are big ones around. The small ones usually don't mix, as they fear they might get eaten. At just over 6 feet (2 m) long, this shark was still big, but small enough to squeeze through the camera windows. As it rushed towards the tuna bait the small fish scattered. We saw the shark's black eye roll back. It took two-thirds of the tuna in its mouth and, shaking its head, careered straight towards the large viewing windows in the cage. Thinking it would crash through the camera ports into the cage, I lunged across the girls' backs and threw my fist towards the shark's gills, hoping to stop its entry. My extended arm didn't quite connect.

Shaking its head from side to side, the shark opened its jaws and took two extra bites right in front of our faces. The big tuna disappeared and the sharp teeth cut through the rope. The shark swam forward into the window, just level with my fist, bashing its tail as it tried to maneuver. The head and long pectoral fin passed through the viewing window; the shark swerved to get free, and with a couple of kicks of its tail, sped off out of sight. The girls' adrenalin must have been pumping. They were breathing faster and were busy making signs and faces at one another. I hoped this incident wouldn't frighten

SHAKING ITS HEAD FROM SIDE TO SIDE, THE SHARK OPENED ITS TOOTHY JAWS AND TOOK TWO EXTRA BITES RIGHT IN FRONT OF OUR FACES.

THEY WERE NOT SHAKING WITH FRIGHT, BUT ROCKING WITH EXCITEMENT ... LOOKING AROUND FOR MORE ACTION!

them or squash their enthusiasm, and make them hate or fear the sharks. I expected they might even want to get out of the cage, but I worried needlessly. They were not shaking with fright, but rocking with excitement. Sharing their adventure together with crazy facial expressions, they were looking around for more action!

Two more enormous great whites circled the cage at close range during the next 15 minutes. Drifting in a cage in a bottomless cold ocean enhanced the excitement. I knew the girls were experiencing the same feelings of wonder and elation that I had always felt when working with these huge predators. Some time later Sarah indicated she was cold. I signaled, "Do you want to go up?" They all nodded their heads.

On the deck of the *Falie* everyone crowded around. Unable to talk underwater, the girls certainly made up for it now. Words were bubbling out of each mouth, like three freshly opened bottles of champagne. The girls especially loved the little shark and called it "Mini Me."

Although I had been on dozens of expeditions to film and study great whites, this expedition was very, very special to me. I relived my own experiences over the years through the children's emotions, reactions, and words.

It was one of the best moments in my life. I knew the adventure, the excitement, and the beauty of the underwater world would be cemented in their hearts and minds. These students will, I hope, pass on my philosophy – let the sharks live!

GLOSSARY

ampullae of Lorenzini
jelly-filled pores on a shark's head that act as receptors to detect electrical fields in the ocean.

berley
material like fish oil or other bait that is put in the water to attract fish.

bulwarks
solid part of a ship's side, like a fence above the level of the deck.

buoyancy jacket
jacket inflated from the scuba tank, used to regulate buoyancy underwater and, in an emergency, to float the diver to the surface.

cartilage
firm, flexible tissue that sharks have in their bodies instead of bone.

crow's nest
lookout area on a boat, secured near the top of the mast.

drop-off
place on the sea bed where the ocean floor drops away to deep water very suddenly.

fish float
buoy used by a diver to secure fish that have been caught while he or she catches more.

IMAX
technique of wide-screen filming that produces an image ten times larger than that of standard film.

laceration
injury to flesh.

leafing
moving from one side to the other in the water, opposite to the way a leaf falls off a tree.

lead belt
weighted belt, with detachable weights, used by divers to regulate buoyancy.

lobster pots
traps for catching lobsters that are left in the water with bait inside.

power head
explosive head attached to a spear gun that explodes on impact.

scuba diving
swimming underwater using a scuba (self-contained underwater breathing apparatus).

sinkhole
underground cavity in limestone that is filled with fresh water.

snorkeling
swimming with a snorkel, a breathing tube.

spear gun
device used to propel a spear head, used for fishing underwater.

starboard
side of a ship to the right, looking towards the front.

stern
back of a boat.

INDEX

This index is arranged alphabetically, word for word. Page numbers in bold type refer to pages with illustrations of the topic.

Aldinga Beach 1, **2**, 6, 8
Aldinga Reef **2**, 23
Alexander, Frank 7
Althorpe Island 14
ampullae of Lorenzini **32**
apex predator 41

Baker, Malcolm 7
Bebe, Mrs., ambulance driver 8
black whaler shark **17**
blue groper 14
Bource, Henri **23**, 26, **27**
bull shark *see* black whaler shark

cage diving 23, **24**, 29, 43, **44**, **45**, 46
Cairns 32
California 29
Catalina Islands 29
chain mail suit **29**, **30**
Clark, Dr. Eugenie **29**
Coral Sea 32
C7 **43**

Dangerous Reef **26**
Dean, Alf **23**, 24, 25, 26, 27
"the drop-off" 2
dusky morwong **2**

Falie **34**, **38**, 40, 41, 42, 43
Farley, Bruce **1**, 6, 7, **14**
filming, underwater
    18, **25**, 29, 31, 34
Flinders Reef 16
food chain **41–42**
Fox, Andrew 42, **43**, **44**, 45

Fox, Kay **10**

Gerkie, Mrs., ambulance driver 8
Glenmorry 24
great white shark **3**, **4-5**, 6, **22**, **23**, 24, 25, 26, **27**, 29, 38, 41, 42, 43, 44, 45, **46**
Greenslade, Tori **39**, 44
Grindal Island 40

Harding, John 16-20
Hopkins Island 38
Horseshoe Reef 10

IMAX film production **29**

Kamines, Ty **40**, 42
King George whiting **14**

lobsters **14**

Memory Cove 24
Miller, Dr. Justin 8
Mini Me 46
monster sharks 4, 5, 23
Mount Gambier 12, 15

National Geographic 31
New Zealand fur seals 41
North Neptune Islands 41

O'Brien, Sarah **39**, 44, 46
Osprey Reef 32

Port Lincoln 26, 38
power head **16**, **17**, **20**

Rankine, Tommy **39**
Rodger, Brian **14**, 23, 26, **27**

scientific expeditions 28, 32
sea lions 23, **26**, 38, **40**
Search for the Great Sharks, film, 29

shark attack 3-5, 14, 23
shark cage 23, **24**, 29, 43, **44**, **45**, 46
shark repellent device 34, **35**, 36-37
sharks
    black whaler (bull) **17**
    blacktip reef 34, 35
    blue **28**, 29, 30
    great white (white pointer) **3**, **4-5**, 6, **22**, **23**, 24, 25, 26, **27**, 29, 38, 41, 42, 43, 44, 45, **46**
    grey reef 34
    grey nurse 18-19, **20**
    hammerhead 32, **33**, 35, 36-37
    tiger 20, **21**
    whaler 16, **20**
    whale 29
    whitetip reef 34
sinkholes 12, 15
South Neptune Islands 41
Spanish mackerel 18-19
spearfishing 2, 10, 14
spearfishing championships **1**, 2
spear guns 1, 15, 16, 19, 20
"SuperTeachers" 38

Taylor, Ron 16, 20, 25
Taylor, Valerie 16, 20

underwater filming
    18, **25**, 29, 31, 34

Wedge Island 24
West Coast, South Australia 23
white pointer shark
    see great white shark
Williams, Laura **39**, **40**, 42, 44

yellowtail kingfish **14**
Yorke Peninsula 14